The contents of this journal are

PERSONAL

and

CONFIDENTIAL.

DO NOT READ.

If found, please return to:

_____

Phone number:

_____

The Strength Training Workout Log

by

Alex Haddox, M.Ed.

Published by

Palladium Education,® Inc.
6520 Platt Avenue, #174
West Hills, CA 91307-3218
PalladiumEducation.com

Copyright © 2016 by Palladium Education,® Inc.

Except as permitted under the Copyright Act of 1976, no part of this book may be reproduced by any electronic or mechanical means in any form including the use of information storage and retrieval systems, without permission in writing from the copyright owner.

Trademarks: "Palladium Education", and the Palladium Education, Inc. logo are trademarks of Palladium Education,® Inc.

ISBN-13:   978-1-939408-37-2

ISBN-10:   1-939408-37-7

To all the coaches who shaped me into the athlete I became.

Sometimes unwillingly.

Well, in all honesty, usually unwillingly.

The Strength Training Workout Log

Table of Contents

How to Use This Log...iii

Sample Log Entry iv

Training Log.. 1-95

Body Composition Log (skinfold)..97

Body Measurements Log 97

Weight Log 99-100

The Strength Training Workout Log

How to Use This Log

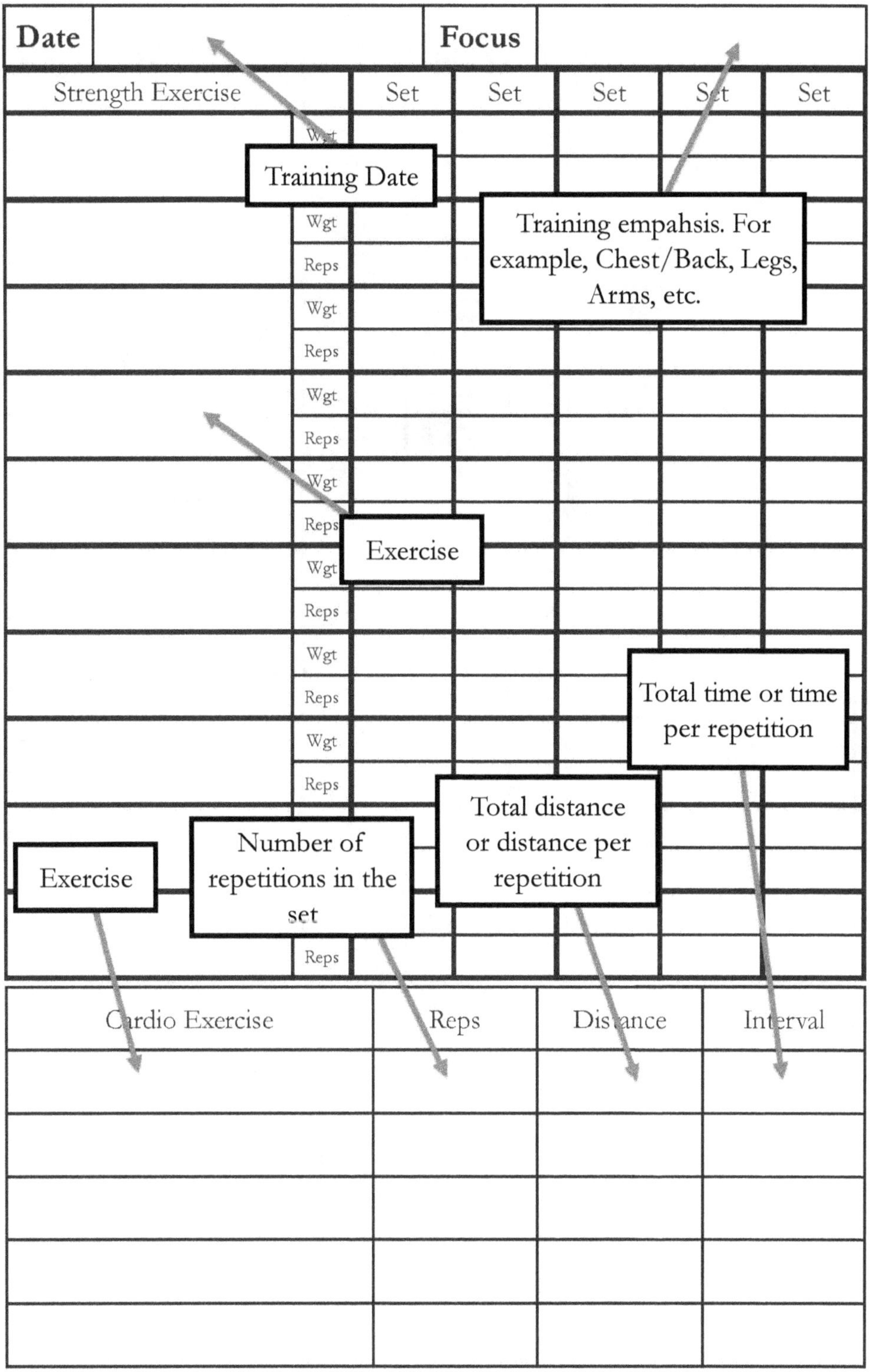

Date			Focus				
Strength Exercise		Set	Set	Set	Set	Set
		Wgt					
		Reps					
		Wgt					
		Reps					
		Wgt					
		Reps					
		Wgt					
		Reps					
		Wgt					
		Reps					
		Wgt					
		Reps					
		Wgt					
		Reps					
		Wgt					
		Reps					
Cardio Exercise			Reps		Distance		Interval

Labels (with arrows pointing to the table):
- Training Date
- Training emphasis. For example, Chest/Back, Legs, Arms, etc.
- Exercise
- Total time or time per repetition
- Number of repetitions in the set
- Total distance or distance per repetition
- Exercise

PalladiumEducation.com

iii

The Strength Training Workout Log

Sample Log Entry

Date	7/14/2016		Focus	ARMS			
Strength Exercise		Set	Set	Set	Set	Set
SKULL CRUSHER	Wgt	35	40	45		
	Reps	16	14	12		
PREACHER	Wgt	45	50	55		
	Reps	16	14	8		
OVERHEAD TRI-EXT	Wgt	25	30	35		
	Reps	14	12	10		
STND RUNNER CURLS	Wgt	35	40	45		
	Reps	16	14	12		
	Wgt					
	Reps					
	Wgt					
	Reps					
	Wgt					
	Reps					
	Wgt					
	Reps					
	Wgt					
	Reps					
	Wgt					
	Reps					

Cardio Exercise	Reps	Distance	Interval
SWIM	3	200	4:00
STATIONARY BIKE	1	7.8m	30:00
HIKE, TRAIL	1	3m	40:00

The Strength Training Workout Log

Date			Focus				
Strength Exercise		Set	Set	Set	Set	Set	

Strength Exercise			Set	Set	Set	Set	Set
	Wgt						
	Reps						
	Wgt						
	Reps						
	Wgt						
	Reps						
	Wgt						
	Reps						
	Wgt						
	Reps						
	Wgt						
	Reps						
	Wgt						
	Reps						
	Wgt						
	Reps						
	Wgt						
	Reps						
	Wgt						
	Reps						

Cardio Exercise	Reps	Distance	Interval

The Strength Training Workout Log

Date			Focus				
Strength Exercise		Set	Set	Set	Set	Set
	Wgt					
	Reps					
	Wgt					
	Reps					
	Wgt					
	Reps					
	Wgt					
	Reps					
	Wgt					
	Reps					
	Wgt					
	Reps					
	Wgt					
	Reps					
	Wgt					
	Reps					
	Wgt					
	Reps					
	Wgt					
	Reps					

Cardio Exercise	Reps	Distance	Interval

Palladium Education,® Inc.

The Strength Training Workout Log

Date			Focus				
Strength Exercise		Set	Set	Set	Set	Set
	Wgt					
	Reps					
	Wgt					
	Reps					
	Wgt					
	Reps					
	Wgt					
	Reps					
	Wgt					
	Reps					
	Wgt					
	Reps					
	Wgt					
	Reps					
	Wgt					
	Reps					
	Wgt					
	Reps					
	Wgt					
	Reps					

Cardio Exercise	Reps	Distance	Interval

The Strength Training Workout Log

Date			Focus		

Strength Exercise		Set	Set	Set	Set	Set
	Wgt					
	Reps					
	Wgt					
	Reps					
	Wgt					
	Reps					
	Wgt					
	Reps					
	Wgt					
	Reps					
	Wgt					
	Reps					
	Wgt					
	Reps					
	Wgt					
	Reps					
	Wgt					
	Reps					
	Wgt					
	Reps					

Cardio Exercise	Reps	Distance	Interval

The Strength Training Workout Log

Date				Focus				
Strength Exercise				Set	Set	Set	Set	Set
			Wgt					
			Reps					
			Wgt					
			Reps					
			Wgt					
			Reps					
			Wgt					
			Reps					
			Wgt					
			Reps					
			Wgt					
			Reps					
			Wgt					
			Reps					
			Wgt					
			Reps					
			Wgt					
			Reps					
			Wgt					
			Reps					

Cardio Exercise	Reps	Distance	Interval

PalladiumEducation.com

The Strength Training Workout Log

Date			Focus				
Strength Exercise		Set	Set	Set	Set	Set	
	Wgt						
	Reps						
	Wgt						
	Reps						
	Wgt						
	Reps						
	Wgt						
	Reps						
	Wgt						
	Reps						
	Wgt						
	Reps						
	Wgt						
	Reps						
	Wgt						
	Reps						
	Wgt						
	Reps						
	Wgt						
	Reps						

Cardio Exercise	Reps	Distance	Interval

The Strength Training Workout Log

Date			Focus				
Strength Exercise		Set	Set	Set	Set	Set
	Wgt					
	Reps					
	Wgt					
	Reps					
	Wgt					
	Reps					
	Wgt					
	Reps					
	Wgt					
	Reps					
	Wgt					
	Reps					
	Wgt					
	Reps					
	Wgt					
	Reps					
	Wgt					
	Reps					
	Wgt					
	Reps					

Cardio Exercise	Reps	Distance	Interval

The Strength Training Workout Log

Date			Focus				
Strength Exercise		Set	Set	Set	Set	Set
	Wgt					
	Reps					
	Wgt					
	Reps					
	Wgt					
	Reps					
	Wgt					
	Reps					
	Wgt					
	Reps					
	Wgt					
	Reps					
	Wgt					
	Reps					
	Wgt					
	Reps					
	Wgt					
	Reps					
	Wgt					
	Reps					

Cardio Exercise	Reps	Distance	Interval

Palladium Education,® Inc.

The Strength Training Workout Log

Date			Focus				
Strength Exercise		Set	Set	Set	Set	Set	
	Wgt						
	Reps						
	Wgt						
	Reps						
	Wgt						
	Reps						
	Wgt						
	Reps						
	Wgt						
	Reps						
	Wgt						
	Reps						
	Wgt						
	Reps						
	Wgt						
	Reps						
	Wgt						
	Reps						
	Wgt						
	Reps						

Cardio Exercise	Reps	Distance	Interval

The Strength Training Workout Log

Date			Focus				
Strength Exercise		Set	Set	Set	Set	Set
	Wgt					
	Reps					
	Wgt					
	Reps					
	Wgt					
	Reps					
	Wgt					
	Reps					
	Wgt					
	Reps					
	Wgt					
	Reps					
	Wgt					
	Reps					
	Wgt					
	Reps					
	Wgt					
	Reps					
	Wgt					
	Reps					

Cardio Exercise	Reps	Distance	Interval

The Strength Training Workout Log

Date			Focus				
Strength Exercise		Set	Set	Set	Set	Set	
	Wgt						
	Reps						
	Wgt						
	Reps						
	Wgt						
	Reps						
	Wgt						
	Reps						
	Wgt						
	Reps						
	Wgt						
	Reps						
	Wgt						
	Reps						
	Wgt						
	Reps						
	Wgt						
	Reps						
	Wgt						
	Reps						

Cardio Exercise	Reps	Distance	Interval

The Strength Training Workout Log

Date			Focus				
Strength Exercise		Set	Set	Set	Set	Set	
	Wgt						
	Reps						
	Wgt						
	Reps						
	Wgt						
	Reps						
	Wgt						
	Reps						
	Wgt						
	Reps						
	Wgt						
	Reps						
	Wgt						
	Reps						
	Wgt						
	Reps						
	Wgt						
	Reps						
	Wgt						
	Reps						

Cardio Exercise	Reps	Distance	Interval

The Strength Training Workout Log

Date			Focus				
Strength Exercise		Set	Set	Set	Set	Set	
	Wgt						
	Reps						
	Wgt						
	Reps						
	Wgt						
	Reps						
	Wgt						
	Reps						
	Wgt						
	Reps						
	Wgt						
	Reps						
	Wgt						
	Reps						
	Wgt						
	Reps						
	Wgt						
	Reps						
	Wgt						
	Reps						

Cardio Exercise	Reps	Distance	Interval

The Strength Training Workout Log

Date			Focus			
Strength Exercise		Set	Set	Set	Set	Set
	Wgt					
	Reps					
	Wgt					
	Reps					
	Wgt					
	Reps					
	Wgt					
	Reps					
	Wgt					
	Reps					
	Wgt					
	Reps					
	Wgt					
	Reps					
	Wgt					
	Reps					
	Wgt					
	Reps					
	Wgt					
	Reps					

Cardio Exercise	Reps	Distance	Interval

The Strength Training Workout Log

Date			Focus				
Strength Exercise		Set	Set	Set	Set	Set	
	Wgt						
	Reps						
	Wgt						
	Reps						
	Wgt						
	Reps						
	Wgt						
	Reps						
	Wgt						
	Reps						
	Wgt						
	Reps						
	Wgt						
	Reps						
	Wgt						
	Reps						
	Wgt						
	Reps						
	Wgt						
	Reps						

Cardio Exercise	Reps	Distance	Interval

The Strength Training Workout Log

Date			Focus				
Strength Exercise		Set	Set	Set	Set	Set
	Wgt					
	Reps					
	Wgt					
	Reps					
	Wgt					
	Reps					
	Wgt					
	Reps					
	Wgt					
	Reps					
	Wgt					
	Reps					
	Wgt					
	Reps					
	Wgt					
	Reps					
	Wgt					
	Reps					
	Wgt					
	Reps					

Cardio Exercise	Reps	Distance	Interval

The Strength Training Workout Log

Date			Focus				
Strength Exercise		Set	Set	Set	Set	Set	
	Wgt						
	Reps						
	Wgt						
	Reps						
	Wgt						
	Reps						
	Wgt						
	Reps						
	Wgt						
	Reps						
	Wgt						
	Reps						
	Wgt						
	Reps						
	Wgt						
	Reps						
	Wgt						
	Reps						
	Wgt						
	Reps						

Cardio Exercise	Reps	Distance	Interval

The Strength Training Workout Log

Date				Focus			
Strength Exercise		Set	Set	Set	Set	Set
	Wgt					
	Reps					
	Wgt					
	Reps					
	Wgt					
	Reps					
	Wgt					
	Reps					
	Wgt					
	Reps					
	Wgt					
	Reps					
	Wgt					
	Reps					
	Wgt					
	Reps					
	Wgt					
	Reps					
	Wgt					
	Reps					

Cardio Exercise	Reps	Distance	Interval

The Strength Training Workout Log

Date				Focus				
Strength Exercise			Set	Set	Set	Set	Set
		Wgt					
		Reps					
		Wgt					
		Reps					
		Wgt					
		Reps					
		Wgt					
		Reps					
		Wgt					
		Reps					
		Wgt					
		Reps					
		Wgt					
		Reps					
		Wgt					
		Reps					
		Wgt					
		Reps					
		Wgt					
		Reps					

Cardio Exercise	Reps	Distance	Interval

The Strength Training Workout Log

Date			Focus				
Strength Exercise		Set	Set	Set	Set	Set
	Wgt					
	Reps					
	Wgt					
	Reps					
	Wgt					
	Reps					
	Wgt					
	Reps					
	Wgt					
	Reps					
	Wgt					
	Reps					
	Wgt					
	Reps					
	Wgt					
	Reps					
	Wgt					
	Reps					
	Wgt					
	Reps					

Cardio Exercise	Reps	Distance	Interval

The Strength Training Workout Log

Date				Focus				
Strength Exercise			Set	Set	Set	Set	Set
		Wgt					
		Reps					
		Wgt					
		Reps					
		Wgt					
		Reps					
		Wgt					
		Reps					
		Wgt					
		Reps					
		Wgt					
		Reps					
		Wgt					
		Reps					
		Wgt					
		Reps					
		Wgt					
		Reps					
		Wgt					
		Reps					

Cardio Exercise	Reps	Distance	Interval

The Strength Training Workout Log

Date			Focus				
Strength Exercise		Set	Set	Set	Set	Set
	Wgt					
	Reps					
	Wgt					
	Reps					
	Wgt					
	Reps					
	Wgt					
	Reps					
	Wgt					
	Reps					
	Wgt					
	Reps					
	Wgt					
	Reps					
	Wgt					
	Reps					
	Wgt					
	Reps					
	Wgt					
	Reps					

Cardio Exercise	Reps	Distance	Interval

The Strength Training Workout Log

Date				Focus				
Strength Exercise			Set	Set	Set	Set	Set
		Wgt					
		Reps					
		Wgt					
		Reps					
		Wgt					
		Reps					
		Wgt					
		Reps					
		Wgt					
		Reps					
		Wgt					
		Reps					
		Wgt					
		Reps					
		Wgt					
		Reps					
		Wgt					
		Reps					
		Wgt					
		Reps					

Cardio Exercise	Reps	Distance	Interval

The Strength Training Workout Log

Date			Focus				
Strength Exercise			Set	Set	Set	Set	Set
		Wgt					
		Reps					
		Wgt					
		Reps					
		Wgt					
		Reps					
		Wgt					
		Reps					
		Wgt					
		Reps					
		Wgt					
		Reps					
		Wgt					
		Reps					
		Wgt					
		Reps					
		Wgt					
		Reps					
		Wgt					
		Reps					

Cardio Exercise	Reps	Distance	Interval

The Strength Training Workout Log

Date			Focus				
Strength Exercise		Set	Set	Set	Set	Set
---	---	---	---	---	---	---
	Wgt					
	Reps					
	Wgt					
	Reps					
	Wgt					
	Reps					
	Wgt					
	Reps					
	Wgt					
	Reps					
	Wgt					
	Reps					
	Wgt					
	Reps					
	Wgt					
	Reps					
	Wgt					
	Reps					
	Wgt					
	Reps					

Cardio Exercise	Reps	Distance	Interval

PalladiumEducation.com

The Strength Training Workout Log

Date			Focus				
Strength Exercise		Set	Set	Set	Set	Set
	Wgt					
	Reps					
	Wgt					
	Reps					
	Wgt					
	Reps					
	Wgt					
	Reps					
	Wgt					
	Reps					
	Wgt					
	Reps					
	Wgt					
	Reps					
	Wgt					
	Reps					
	Wgt					
	Reps					
	Wgt					
	Reps					

Cardio Exercise	Reps	Distance	Interval

The Strength Training Workout Log

Date				Focus			
Strength Exercise		Set	Set	Set	Set	Set
	Wgt					
	Reps					
	Wgt					
	Reps					
	Wgt					
	Reps					
	Wgt					
	Reps					
	Wgt					
	Reps					
	Wgt					
	Reps					
	Wgt					
	Reps					
	Wgt					
	Reps					
	Wgt					
	Reps					
	Wgt					
	Reps					

Cardio Exercise	Reps	Distance	Interval

The Strength Training Workout Log

Date			Focus			

Strength Exercise		Set	Set	Set	Set	Set
	Wgt					
	Reps					
	Wgt					
	Reps					
	Wgt					
	Reps					
	Wgt					
	Reps					
	Wgt					
	Reps					
	Wgt					
	Reps					
	Wgt					
	Reps					
	Wgt					
	Reps					
	Wgt					
	Reps					
	Wgt					
	Reps					

Cardio Exercise	Reps	Distance	Interval

The Strength Training Workout Log

Date			Focus				
Strength Exercise			Set	Set	Set	Set	Set
		Wgt					
		Reps					
		Wgt					
		Reps					
		Wgt					
		Reps					
		Wgt					
		Reps					
		Wgt					
		Reps					
		Wgt					
		Reps					
		Wgt					
		Reps					
		Wgt					
		Reps					
		Wgt					
		Reps					
		Wgt					
		Reps					

Cardio Exercise	Reps	Distance	Interval

The Strength Training Workout Log

Date			Focus				
Strength Exercise		Set	Set	Set	Set	Set	
	Wgt						
	Reps						
	Wgt						
	Reps						
	Wgt						
	Reps						
	Wgt						
	Reps						
	Wgt						
	Reps						
	Wgt						
	Reps						
	Wgt						
	Reps						
	Wgt						
	Reps						
	Wgt						
	Reps						
	Wgt						
	Reps						

Cardio Exercise	Reps	Distance	Interval

The Strength Training Workout Log

Date				Focus			
Strength Exercise		Set	Set	Set	Set	Set
	Wgt					
	Reps					
	Wgt					
	Reps					
	Wgt					
	Reps					
	Wgt					
	Reps					
	Wgt					
	Reps					
	Wgt					
	Reps					
	Wgt					
	Reps					
	Wgt					
	Reps					
	Wgt					
	Reps					
	Wgt					
	Reps					

Cardio Exercise	Reps	Distance	Interval

The Strength Training Workout Log

Date			Focus				
Strength Exercise		Set	Set	Set	Set	Set
	Wgt					
	Reps					
	Wgt					
	Reps					
	Wgt					
	Reps					
	Wgt					
	Reps					
	Wgt					
	Reps					
	Wgt					
	Reps					
	Wgt					
	Reps					
	Wgt					
	Reps					
	Wgt					
	Reps					
	Wgt					
	Reps					

Cardio Exercise	Reps	Distance	Interval

The Strength Training Workout Log

Date				Focus			
Strength Exercise		Set	Set	Set	Set	Set
	Wgt					
	Reps					
	Wgt					
	Reps					
	Wgt					
	Reps					
	Wgt					
	Reps					
	Wgt					
	Reps					
	Wgt					
	Reps					
	Wgt					
	Reps					
	Wgt					
	Reps					
	Wgt					
	Reps					
	Wgt					
	Reps					

Cardio Exercise	Reps	Distance	Interval

PalladiumEducation.com

The Strength Training Workout Log

Date			Focus			
Strength Exercise		Set	Set	Set	Set	Set
	Wgt					
	Reps					
	Wgt					
	Reps					
	Wgt					
	Reps					
	Wgt					
	Reps					
	Wgt					
	Reps					
	Wgt					
	Reps					
	Wgt					
	Reps					
	Wgt					
	Reps					
	Wgt					
	Reps					
	Wgt					
	Reps					

Cardio Exercise	Reps	Distance	Interval

The Strength Training Workout Log

Date			Focus				
Strength Exercise			Set	Set	Set	Set	Set
		Wgt					
		Reps					
		Wgt					
		Reps					
		Wgt					
		Reps					
		Wgt					
		Reps					
		Wgt					
		Reps					
		Wgt					
		Reps					
		Wgt					
		Reps					
		Wgt					
		Reps					
		Wgt					
		Reps					
		Wgt					
		Reps					

Cardio Exercise	Reps	Distance	Interval

The Strength Training Workout Log

Date			Focus			

Strength Exercise		Set	Set	Set	Set	Set
	Wgt					
	Reps					
	Wgt					
	Reps					
	Wgt					
	Reps					
	Wgt					
	Reps					
	Wgt					
	Reps					
	Wgt					
	Reps					
	Wgt					
	Reps					
	Wgt					
	Reps					
	Wgt					
	Reps					
	Wgt					
	Reps					

Cardio Exercise	Reps	Distance	Interval

The Strength Training Workout Log

Date		Focus				
Strength Exercise		Set	Set	Set	Set	Set
	Wgt					
	Reps					
	Wgt					
	Reps					
	Wgt					
	Reps					
	Wgt					
	Reps					
	Wgt					
	Reps					
	Wgt					
	Reps					
	Wgt					
	Reps					
	Wgt					
	Reps					
	Wgt					
	Reps					
	Wgt					
	Reps					

Cardio Exercise	Reps	Distance	Interval

PalladiumEducation.com

The Strength Training Workout Log

Date			Focus			

Strength Exercise		Set	Set	Set	Set	Set
	Wgt					
	Reps					
	Wgt					
	Reps					
	Wgt					
	Reps					
	Wgt					
	Reps					
	Wgt					
	Reps					
	Wgt					
	Reps					
	Wgt					
	Reps					
	Wgt					
	Reps					
	Wgt					
	Reps					
	Wgt					
	Reps					

Cardio Exercise	Reps	Distance	Interval

The Strength Training Workout Log

Date				Focus			
Strength Exercise		Set	Set	Set	Set	Set
---	---	---	---	---	---	---
	Wgt					
	Reps					
	Wgt					
	Reps					
	Wgt					
	Reps					
	Wgt					
	Reps					
	Wgt					
	Reps					
	Wgt					
	Reps					
	Wgt					
	Reps					
	Wgt					
	Reps					
	Wgt					
	Reps					
	Wgt					
	Reps					

Cardio Exercise	Reps	Distance	Interval

The Strength Training Workout Log

Date			Focus			
Strength Exercise		Set	Set	Set	Set	Set
	Wgt					
	Reps					
	Wgt					
	Reps					
	Wgt					
	Reps					
	Wgt					
	Reps					
	Wgt					
	Reps					
	Wgt					
	Reps					
	Wgt					
	Reps					
	Wgt					
	Reps					
	Wgt					
	Reps					
	Wgt					
	Reps					

Cardio Exercise	Reps	Distance	Interval

The Strength Training Workout Log

Date				Focus				
Strength Exercise			Set	Set	Set	Set	Set
		Wgt					
		Reps					
		Wgt					
		Reps					
		Wgt					
		Reps					
		Wgt					
		Reps					
		Wgt					
		Reps					
		Wgt					
		Reps					
		Wgt					
		Reps					
		Wgt					
		Reps					
		Wgt					
		Reps					
		Wgt					
		Reps					

Cardio Exercise	Reps	Distance	Interval

The Strength Training Workout Log

Date			Focus				
Strength Exercise		Set	Set	Set	Set	Set
	Wgt					
	Reps					
	Wgt					
	Reps					
	Wgt					
	Reps					
	Wgt					
	Reps					
	Wgt					
	Reps					
	Wgt					
	Reps					
	Wgt					
	Reps					
	Wgt					
	Reps					
	Wgt					
	Reps					
	Wgt					
	Reps					

Cardio Exercise	Reps	Distance	Interval

Palladium Education,® Inc.

The Strength Training Workout Log

Date			Focus		
Strength Exercise		Set	Set	Set	Set	Set

Strength Exercise		Set	Set	Set	Set	Set
	Wgt					
	Reps					
	Wgt					
	Reps					
	Wgt					
	Reps					
	Wgt					
	Reps					
	Wgt					
	Reps					
	Wgt					
	Reps					
	Wgt					
	Reps					
	Wgt					
	Reps					
	Wgt					
	Reps					
	Wgt					
	Reps					

Cardio Exercise	Reps	Distance	Interval

The Strength Training Workout Log

Date			Focus			

Strength Exercise		Set	Set	Set	Set	Set
	Wgt					
	Reps					
	Wgt					
	Reps					
	Wgt					
	Reps					
	Wgt					
	Reps					
	Wgt					
	Reps					
	Wgt					
	Reps					
	Wgt					
	Reps					
	Wgt					
	Reps					
	Wgt					
	Reps					
	Wgt					
	Reps					

Cardio Exercise	Reps	Distance	Interval

Palladium Education,® Inc.

The Strength Training Workout Log

Date			Focus				
Strength Exercise		Set	Set	Set	Set	Set	

Strength Exercise						
	Wgt					
	Reps					
	Wgt					
	Reps					
	Wgt					
	Reps					
	Wgt					
	Reps					
	Wgt					
	Reps					
	Wgt					
	Reps					
	Wgt					
	Reps					
	Wgt					
	Reps					
	Wgt					
	Reps					
	Wgt					
	Reps					

Cardio Exercise	Reps	Distance	Interval

The Strength Training Workout Log

Date			Focus			

Strength Exercise		Set	Set	Set	Set	Set
	Wgt					
	Reps					
	Wgt					
	Reps					
	Wgt					
	Reps					
	Wgt					
	Reps					
	Wgt					
	Reps					
	Wgt					
	Reps					
	Wgt					
	Reps					
	Wgt					
	Reps					
	Wgt					
	Reps					
	Wgt					
	Reps					

Cardio Exercise	Reps	Distance	Interval

The Strength Training Workout Log

Date			Focus				
Strength Exercise			Set	Set	Set	Set	Set
		Wgt					
		Reps					
		Wgt					
		Reps					
		Wgt					
		Reps					
		Wgt					
		Reps					
		Wgt					
		Reps					
		Wgt					
		Reps					
		Wgt					
		Reps					
		Wgt					
		Reps					
		Wgt					
		Reps					
		Wgt					
		Reps					

Cardio Exercise	Reps	Distance	Interval

PalladiumEducation.com

The Strength Training Workout Log

Date			Focus				
Strength Exercise		Set	Set	Set	Set	Set
---	---	---	---	---	---	---
	Wgt					
	Reps					
	Wgt					
	Reps					
	Wgt					
	Reps					
	Wgt					
	Reps					
	Wgt					
	Reps					
	Wgt					
	Reps					
	Wgt					
	Reps					
	Wgt					
	Reps					
	Wgt					
	Reps					
	Wgt					
	Reps					

Cardio Exercise	Reps	Distance	Interval

The Strength Training Workout Log

Date			Focus			
Strength Exercise		Set	Set	Set	Set	Set
	Wgt					
	Reps					
	Wgt					
	Reps					
	Wgt					
	Reps					
	Wgt					
	Reps					
	Wgt					
	Reps					
	Wgt					
	Reps					
	Wgt					
	Reps					
	Wgt					
	Reps					
	Wgt					
	Reps					
	Wgt					
	Reps					

Cardio Exercise	Reps	Distance	Interval

The Strength Training Workout Log

Date				Focus				
Strength Exercise			Set	Set	Set	Set	Set
		Wgt					
		Reps					
		Wgt					
		Reps					
		Wgt					
		Reps					
		Wgt					
		Reps					
		Wgt					
		Reps					
		Wgt					
		Reps					
		Wgt					
		Reps					
		Wgt					
		Reps					
		Wgt					
		Reps					
		Wgt					
		Reps					

Cardio Exercise	Reps	Distance	Interval

The Strength Training Workout Log

Date			Focus				
Strength Exercise		Set	Set	Set	Set	Set	
		Wgt					
		Reps					
		Wgt					
		Reps					
		Wgt					
		Reps					
		Wgt					
		Reps					
		Wgt					
		Reps					
		Wgt					
		Reps					
		Wgt					
		Reps					
		Wgt					
		Reps					
		Wgt					
		Reps					
		Wgt					
		Reps					

Cardio Exercise	Reps	Distance	Interval

The Strength Training Workout Log

Date			Focus		

Strength Exercise		Set	Set	Set	Set	Set
	Wgt					
	Reps					
	Wgt					
	Reps					
	Wgt					
	Reps					
	Wgt					
	Reps					
	Wgt					
	Reps					
	Wgt					
	Reps					
	Wgt					
	Reps					
	Wgt					
	Reps					
	Wgt					
	Reps					
	Wgt					
	Reps					

Cardio Exercise	Reps	Distance	Interval

The Strength Training Workout Log

Date			Focus				
Strength Exercise		Set	Set	Set	Set	Set
---	---	---	---	---	---	---
	Wgt					
	Reps					
	Wgt					
	Reps					
	Wgt					
	Reps					
	Wgt					
	Reps					
	Wgt					
	Reps					
	Wgt					
	Reps					
	Wgt					
	Reps					
	Wgt					
	Reps					
	Wgt					
	Reps					
	Wgt					
	Reps					

Cardio Exercise	Reps	Distance	Interval

The Strength Training Workout Log

Date			Focus				
Strength Exercise			Set	Set	Set	Set	Set
		Wgt					
		Reps					
		Wgt					
		Reps					
		Wgt					
		Reps					
		Wgt					
		Reps					
		Wgt					
		Reps					
		Wgt					
		Reps					
		Wgt					
		Reps					
		Wgt					
		Reps					
		Wgt					
		Reps					
		Wgt					
		Reps					

Cardio Exercise	Reps	Distance	Interval

The Strength Training Workout Log

Date			Focus				
Strength Exercise		Set	Set	Set	Set	Set	
	Wgt						
	Reps						
	Wgt						
	Reps						
	Wgt						
	Reps						
	Wgt						
	Reps						
	Wgt						
	Reps						
	Wgt						
	Reps						
	Wgt						
	Reps						
	Wgt						
	Reps						
	Wgt						
	Reps						
	Wgt						
	Reps						

Cardio Exercise	Reps	Distance	Interval

The Strength Training Workout Log

Date			Focus			
Strength Exercise		Set	Set	Set	Set	Set
	Wgt					
	Reps					
	Wgt					
	Reps					
	Wgt					
	Reps					
	Wgt					
	Reps					
	Wgt					
	Reps					
	Wgt					
	Reps					
	Wgt					
	Reps					
	Wgt					
	Reps					
	Wgt					
	Reps					
	Wgt					
	Reps					

Cardio Exercise	Reps	Distance	Interval

The Strength Training Workout Log

Date				Focus			
Strength Exercise		Set	Set	Set	Set	Set
		Wgt					
		Reps					
		Wgt					
		Reps					
		Wgt					
		Reps					
		Wgt					
		Reps					
		Wgt					
		Reps					
		Wgt					
		Reps					
		Wgt					
		Reps					
		Wgt					
		Reps					
		Wgt					
		Reps					
		Wgt					
		Reps					

Cardio Exercise	Reps	Distance	Interval

PalladiumEducation.com

The Strength Training Workout Log

Date			Focus				
Strength Exercise			Set	Set	Set	Set	Set
		Wgt					
		Reps					
		Wgt					
		Reps					
		Wgt					
		Reps					
		Wgt					
		Reps					
		Wgt					
		Reps					
		Wgt					
		Reps					
		Wgt					
		Reps					
		Wgt					
		Reps					
		Wgt					
		Reps					
		Wgt					
		Reps					

Cardio Exercise	Reps	Distance	Interval

The Strength Training Workout Log

Date				Focus			
Strength Exercise		Set	Set	Set	Set	Set
	Wgt					
	Reps					
	Wgt					
	Reps					
	Wgt					
	Reps					
	Wgt					
	Reps					
	Wgt					
	Reps					
	Wgt					
	Reps					
	Wgt					
	Reps					
	Wgt					
	Reps					
	Wgt					
	Reps					
	Wgt					
	Reps					

Cardio Exercise	Reps	Distance	Interval

The Strength Training Workout Log

Date			Focus				
Strength Exercise		Set	Set	Set	Set	Set
	Wgt					
	Reps					
	Wgt					
	Reps					
	Wgt					
	Reps					
	Wgt					
	Reps					
	Wgt					
	Reps					
	Wgt					
	Reps					
	Wgt					
	Reps					
	Wgt					
	Reps					
	Wgt					
	Reps					
	Wgt					
	Reps					

Cardio Exercise	Reps	Distance	Interval

The Strength Training Workout Log

Date				Focus				
Strength Exercise			Set	Set	Set	Set	Set
		Wgt					
		Reps					
		Wgt					
		Reps					
		Wgt					
		Reps					
		Wgt					
		Reps					
		Wgt					
		Reps					
		Wgt					
		Reps					
		Wgt					
		Reps					
		Wgt					
		Reps					
		Wgt					
		Reps					
		Wgt					
		Reps					

Cardio Exercise	Reps	Distance	Interval

The Strength Training Workout Log

Date			Focus				
Strength Exercise		Set	Set	Set	Set	Set	
	Wgt						
	Reps						
	Wgt						
	Reps						
	Wgt						
	Reps						
	Wgt						
	Reps						
	Wgt						
	Reps						
	Wgt						
	Reps						
	Wgt						
	Reps						
	Wgt						
	Reps						
	Wgt						
	Reps						
	Wgt						
	Reps						

Cardio Exercise	Reps	Distance	Interval

The Strength Training Workout Log

Date				Focus			
Strength Exercise		Set	Set	Set	Set	Set
		Wgt					
		Reps					
		Wgt					
		Reps					
		Wgt					
		Reps					
		Wgt					
		Reps					
		Wgt					
		Reps					
		Wgt					
		Reps					
		Wgt					
		Reps					
		Wgt					
		Reps					
		Wgt					
		Reps					
		Wgt					
		Reps					

Cardio Exercise	Reps	Distance	Interval

The Strength Training Workout Log

Date			Focus				
Strength Exercise		Set	Set	Set	Set	Set
---	---	---	---	---	---	---
	Wgt					
	Reps					
	Wgt					
	Reps					
	Wgt					
	Reps					
	Wgt					
	Reps					
	Wgt					
	Reps					
	Wgt					
	Reps					
	Wgt					
	Reps					
	Wgt					
	Reps					
	Wgt					
	Reps					
	Wgt					
	Reps					

Cardio Exercise	Reps	Distance	Interval

The Strength Training Workout Log

Date				Focus				
Strength Exercise			Set	Set	Set	Set	Set
		Wgt					
		Reps					
		Wgt					
		Reps					
		Wgt					
		Reps					
		Wgt					
		Reps					
		Wgt					
		Reps					
		Wgt					
		Reps					
		Wgt					
		Reps					
		Wgt					
		Reps					
		Wgt					
		Reps					
		Wgt					
		Reps					

Cardio Exercise	Reps	Distance	Interval

The Strength Training Workout Log

Date			Focus				

Strength Exercise		Set	Set	Set	Set	Set
	Wgt					
	Reps					
	Wgt					
	Reps					
	Wgt					
	Reps					
	Wgt					
	Reps					
	Wgt					
	Reps					
	Wgt					
	Reps					
	Wgt					
	Reps					
	Wgt					
	Reps					
	Wgt					
	Reps					
	Wgt					
	Reps					

Cardio Exercise	Reps	Distance	Interval

The Strength Training Workout Log

Date			Focus				
Strength Exercise		Set	Set	Set	Set	Set
	Wgt					
	Reps					
	Wgt					
	Reps					
	Wgt					
	Reps					
	Wgt					
	Reps					
	Wgt					
	Reps					
	Wgt					
	Reps					
	Wgt					
	Reps					
	Wgt					
	Reps					
	Wgt					
	Reps					
	Wgt					
	Reps					

Cardio Exercise	Reps	Distance	Interval

The Strength Training Workout Log

Date			Focus				
Strength Exercise		Set	Set	Set	Set	Set	
	Wgt						
	Reps						
	Wgt						
	Reps						
	Wgt						
	Reps						
	Wgt						
	Reps						
	Wgt						
	Reps						
	Wgt						
	Reps						
	Wgt						
	Reps						
	Wgt						
	Reps						
	Wgt						
	Reps						
	Wgt						
	Reps						

Cardio Exercise	Reps	Distance	Interval

Palladium Education,® Inc.

The Strength Training Workout Log

Date				Focus			
Strength Exercise		Set	Set	Set	Set	Set
	Wgt					
	Reps					
	Wgt					
	Reps					
	Wgt					
	Reps					
	Wgt					
	Reps					
	Wgt					
	Reps					
	Wgt					
	Reps					
	Wgt					
	Reps					
	Wgt					
	Reps					
	Wgt					
	Reps					
	Wgt					
	Reps					

Cardio Exercise	Reps	Distance	Interval

PalladiumEducation.com

The Strength Training Workout Log

Date			Focus			
Strength Exercise		Set	Set	Set	Set	Set
	Wgt					
	Reps					
	Wgt					
	Reps					
	Wgt					
	Reps					
	Wgt					
	Reps					
	Wgt					
	Reps					
	Wgt					
	Reps					
	Wgt					
	Reps					
	Wgt					
	Reps					
	Wgt					
	Reps					
	Wgt					
	Reps					

Cardio Exercise	Reps	Distance	Interval

The Strength Training Workout Log

Date			Focus				
Strength Exercise		Set	Set	Set	Set	Set
	Wgt					
	Reps					
	Wgt					
	Reps					
	Wgt					
	Reps					
	Wgt					
	Reps					
	Wgt					
	Reps					
	Wgt					
	Reps					
	Wgt					
	Reps					
	Wgt					
	Reps					
	Wgt					
	Reps					
	Wgt					
	Reps					

Cardio Exercise	Reps	Distance	Interval

PalladiumEducation.com

The Strength Training Workout Log

Date			Focus				
Strength Exercise		Set	Set	Set	Set	Set
	Wgt					
	Reps					
	Wgt					
	Reps					
	Wgt					
	Reps					
	Wgt					
	Reps					
	Wgt					
	Reps					
	Wgt					
	Reps					
	Wgt					
	Reps					
	Wgt					
	Reps					
	Wgt					
	Reps					
	Wgt					
	Reps					

Cardio Exercise	Reps	Distance	Interval

The Strength Training Workout Log

Date			Focus				
Strength Exercise		Set	Set	Set	Set	Set
	Wgt					
	Reps					
	Wgt					
	Reps					
	Wgt					
	Reps					
	Wgt					
	Reps					
	Wgt					
	Reps					
	Wgt					
	Reps					
	Wgt					
	Reps					
	Wgt					
	Reps					
	Wgt					
	Reps					
	Wgt					
	Reps					

Cardio Exercise	Reps	Distance	Interval

The Strength Training Workout Log

Date			Focus				
Strength Exercise			Set	Set	Set	Set	Set
	Wgt					
	Reps					
	Wgt					
	Reps					
	Wgt					
	Reps					
	Wgt					
	Reps					
	Wgt					
	Reps					
	Wgt					
	Reps					
	Wgt					
	Reps					
	Wgt					
	Reps					
	Wgt					
	Reps					
	Wgt					
	Reps					

Cardio Exercise	Reps	Distance	Interval

The Strength Training Workout Log

Date			Focus				
Strength Exercise		Set	Set	Set	Set	Set
	Wgt					
	Reps					
	Wgt					
	Reps					
	Wgt					
	Reps					
	Wgt					
	Reps					
	Wgt					
	Reps					
	Wgt					
	Reps					
	Wgt					
	Reps					
	Wgt					
	Reps					
	Wgt					
	Reps					
	Wgt					
	Reps					

Cardio Exercise	Reps	Distance	Interval

PalladiumEducation.com

The Strength Training Workout Log

Date			Focus				
Strength Exercise		Set	Set	Set	Set	Set
	Wgt					
	Reps					
	Wgt					
	Reps					
	Wgt					
	Reps					
	Wgt					
	Reps					
	Wgt					
	Reps					
	Wgt					
	Reps					
	Wgt					
	Reps					
	Wgt					
	Reps					
	Wgt					
	Reps					
	Wgt					
	Reps					

Cardio Exercise	Reps	Distance	Interval

The Strength Training Workout Log

Date			Focus				
Strength Exercise		Set	Set	Set	Set	Set
	Wgt					
	Reps					
	Wgt					
	Reps					
	Wgt					
	Reps					
	Wgt					
	Reps					
	Wgt					
	Reps					
	Wgt					
	Reps					
	Wgt					
	Reps					
	Wgt					
	Reps					
	Wgt					
	Reps					
	Wgt					
	Reps					

Cardio Exercise	Reps	Distance	Interval

PalladiumEducation.com

The Strength Training Workout Log

Date			Focus				
Strength Exercise		Set	Set	Set	Set	Set
---	---	---	---	---	---	---
	Wgt					
	Reps					
	Wgt					
	Reps					
	Wgt					
	Reps					
	Wgt					
	Reps					
	Wgt					
	Reps					
	Wgt					
	Reps					
	Wgt					
	Reps					
	Wgt					
	Reps					
	Wgt					
	Reps					
	Wgt					
	Reps					

Cardio Exercise	Reps	Distance	Interval

The Strength Training Workout Log

Date			Focus				
Strength Exercise			Set	Set	Set	Set	Set
		Wgt					
		Reps					
		Wgt					
		Reps					
		Wgt					
		Reps					
		Wgt					
		Reps					
		Wgt					
		Reps					
		Wgt					
		Reps					
		Wgt					
		Reps					
		Wgt					
		Reps					
		Wgt					
		Reps					
		Wgt					
		Reps					

Cardio Exercise	Reps	Distance	Interval

The Strength Training Workout Log

Date				Focus			
Strength Exercise		Set	Set	Set	Set	Set
	Wgt					
	Reps					
	Wgt					
	Reps					
	Wgt					
	Reps					
	Wgt					
	Reps					
	Wgt					
	Reps					
	Wgt					
	Reps					
	Wgt					
	Reps					
	Wgt					
	Reps					
	Wgt					
	Reps					
	Wgt					
	Reps					

Cardio Exercise	Reps	Distance	Interval

The Strength Training Workout Log

Date			Focus					
Strength Exercise			Set	Set	Set	Set	Set
---	---	---	---	---	---	---	---
		Wgt					
		Reps					
		Wgt					
		Reps					
		Wgt					
		Reps					
		Wgt					
		Reps					
		Wgt					
		Reps					
		Wgt					
		Reps					
		Wgt					
		Reps					
		Wgt					
		Reps					
		Wgt					
		Reps					
		Wgt					
		Reps					

Cardio Exercise	Reps	Distance	Interval

The Strength Training Workout Log

Date			Focus				
Strength Exercise		Set	Set	Set	Set	Set
---	---	---	---	---	---	---
	Wgt					
	Reps					
	Wgt					
	Reps					
	Wgt					
	Reps					
	Wgt					
	Reps					
	Wgt					
	Reps					
	Wgt					
	Reps					
	Wgt					
	Reps					
	Wgt					
	Reps					
	Wgt					
	Reps					
	Wgt					
	Reps					

Cardio Exercise	Reps	Distance	Interval

The Strength Training Workout Log

Date			Focus				
Strength Exercise			Set	Set	Set	Set	Set
		Wgt					
		Reps					
		Wgt					
		Reps					
		Wgt					
		Reps					
		Wgt					
		Reps					
		Wgt					
		Reps					
		Wgt					
		Reps					
		Wgt					
		Reps					
		Wgt					
		Reps					
		Wgt					
		Reps					
		Wgt					
		Reps					

Cardio Exercise	Reps	Distance	Interval

PalladiumEducation.com

The Strength Training Workout Log

Date			Focus				
Strength Exercise			Set	Set	Set	Set	Set
		Wgt					
		Reps					
		Wgt					
		Reps					
		Wgt					
		Reps					
		Wgt					
		Reps					
		Wgt					
		Reps					
		Wgt					
		Reps					
		Wgt					
		Reps					
		Wgt					
		Reps					
		Wgt					
		Reps					
		Wgt					
		Reps					

Cardio Exercise	Reps	Distance	Interval

The Strength Training Workout Log

Date			Focus		

Strength Exercise		Set	Set	Set	Set	Set
	Wgt					
	Reps					
	Wgt					
	Reps					
	Wgt					
	Reps					
	Wgt					
	Reps					
	Wgt					
	Reps					
	Wgt					
	Reps					
	Wgt					
	Reps					
	Wgt					
	Reps					
	Wgt					
	Reps					
	Wgt					
	Reps					

Cardio Exercise	Reps	Distance	Interval

PalladiumEducation.com

The Strength Training Workout Log

Date			Focus				
Strength Exercise		Set	Set	Set	Set	Set
---	---	---	---	---	---	---
	Wgt					
	Reps					
	Wgt					
	Reps					
	Wgt					
	Reps					
	Wgt					
	Reps					
	Wgt					
	Reps					
	Wgt					
	Reps					
	Wgt					
	Reps					
	Wgt					
	Reps					
	Wgt					
	Reps					
	Wgt					
	Reps					

Cardio Exercise	Reps	Distance	Interval

The Strength Training Workout Log

Date			Focus		

Strength Exercise		Set	Set	Set	Set	Set
	Wgt					
	Reps					
	Wgt					
	Reps					
	Wgt					
	Reps					
	Wgt					
	Reps					
	Wgt					
	Reps					
	Wgt					
	Reps					
	Wgt					
	Reps					
	Wgt					
	Reps					
	Wgt					
	Reps					
	Wgt					
	Reps					

Cardio Exercise	Reps	Distance	Interval

PalladiumEducation.com

The Strength Training Workout Log

Date		Focus	

Strength Exercise		Set	Set	Set	Set	Set
	Wgt					
	Reps					
	Wgt					
	Reps					
	Wgt					
	Reps					
	Wgt					
	Reps					
	Wgt					
	Reps					
	Wgt					
	Reps					
	Wgt					
	Reps					
	Wgt					
	Reps					
	Wgt					
	Reps					
	Wgt					
	Reps					

Cardio Exercise	Reps	Distance	Interval

The Strength Training Workout Log

Date							
Focus							

Strength Exercise		Set	Set	Set	Set	Set
	Wgt					
	Reps					
	Wgt					
	Reps					
	Wgt					
	Reps					
	Wgt					
	Reps					
	Wgt					
	Reps					
	Wgt					
	Reps					
	Wgt					
	Reps					
	Wgt					
	Reps					
	Wgt					
	Reps					
	Wgt					
	Reps					

Cardio Exercise	Reps	Distance	Interval

The Strength Training Workout Log

Date			Focus				
Strength Exercise			Set	Set	Set	Set	Set
		Wgt					
		Reps					
		Wgt					
		Reps					
		Wgt					
		Reps					
		Wgt					
		Reps					
		Wgt					
		Reps					
		Wgt					
		Reps					
		Wgt					
		Reps					
		Wgt					
		Reps					
		Wgt					
		Reps					
		Wgt					
		Reps					

Cardio Exercise	Reps	Distance	Interval

The Strength Training Workout Log

Date			Focus				
Strength Exercise			Set	Set	Set	Set	Set
		Wgt					
		Reps					
		Wgt					
		Reps					
		Wgt					
		Reps					
		Wgt					
		Reps					
		Wgt					
		Reps					
		Wgt					
		Reps					
		Wgt					
		Reps					
		Wgt					
		Reps					
		Wgt					
		Reps					
		Wgt					
		Reps					

Cardio Exercise	Reps	Distance	Interval

PalladiumEducation.com

The Strength Training Workout Log

Date			Focus				
Strength Exercise		Set	Set	Set	Set	Set	
	Wgt						
	Reps						
	Wgt						
	Reps						
	Wgt						
	Reps						
	Wgt						
	Reps						
	Wgt						
	Reps						
	Wgt						
	Reps						
	Wgt						
	Reps						
	Wgt						
	Reps						
	Wgt						
	Reps						
	Wgt						
	Reps						

Cardio Exercise	Reps	Distance	Interval

Palladium Education,® Inc.

The Strength Training Workout Log

Date			Focus				
Strength Exercise		Set	Set	Set	Set	Set	
	Wgt						
	Reps						
	Wgt						
	Reps						
	Wgt						
	Reps						
	Wgt						
	Reps						
	Wgt						
	Reps						
	Wgt						
	Reps						
	Wgt						
	Reps						
	Wgt						
	Reps						
	Wgt						
	Reps						
	Wgt						
	Reps						

Cardio Exercise	Reps	Distance	Interval

The Strength Training Workout Log

Date			Focus				
Strength Exercise			Set	Set	Set	Set	Set
		Wgt					
		Reps					
		Wgt					
		Reps					
		Wgt					
		Reps					
		Wgt					
		Reps					
		Wgt					
		Reps					
		Wgt					
		Reps					
		Wgt					
		Reps					
		Wgt					
		Reps					
		Wgt					
		Reps					
		Wgt					
		Reps					

Cardio Exercise	Reps	Distance	Interval

The Strength Training Workout Log

Date			Focus				
Strength Exercise			Set	Set	Set	Set	Set
		Wgt					
		Reps					
		Wgt					
		Reps					
		Wgt					
		Reps					
		Wgt					
		Reps					
		Wgt					
		Reps					
		Wgt					
		Reps					
		Wgt					
		Reps					
		Wgt					
		Reps					
		Wgt					
		Reps					
		Wgt					
		Reps					

Cardio Exercise	Reps	Distance	Interval

PalladiumEducation.com

The Strength Training Workout Log

Body Composition Log (skinfold) Measurements are in milimeters (mm)

Date	%	Triceps	Thigh	Suprailiac	Pectoral	Subscapula	Midaxilla	Abdomen

Body Measurements Log

Date	Neck	Chest	L. Arm	Abdomen	Hips	L. Thigh	L. Calf

Weight Log

Date	Weight	Date	Weight

Weight Log

Date	Weight	Date	Weight

www.ingramcontent.com/pod-product-compliance
Lightning Source LLC
Chambersburg PA
CBHW071302040426
42444CB00009B/1843